Where Does It Hurt?

Seed Learning

Where does it hurt?

My head.

My head hurts.

Where does it hurt?

My tummy.

My tummy hurts.

Where does it hurt?

My throat.

My throat hurts.

Where does it hurt?

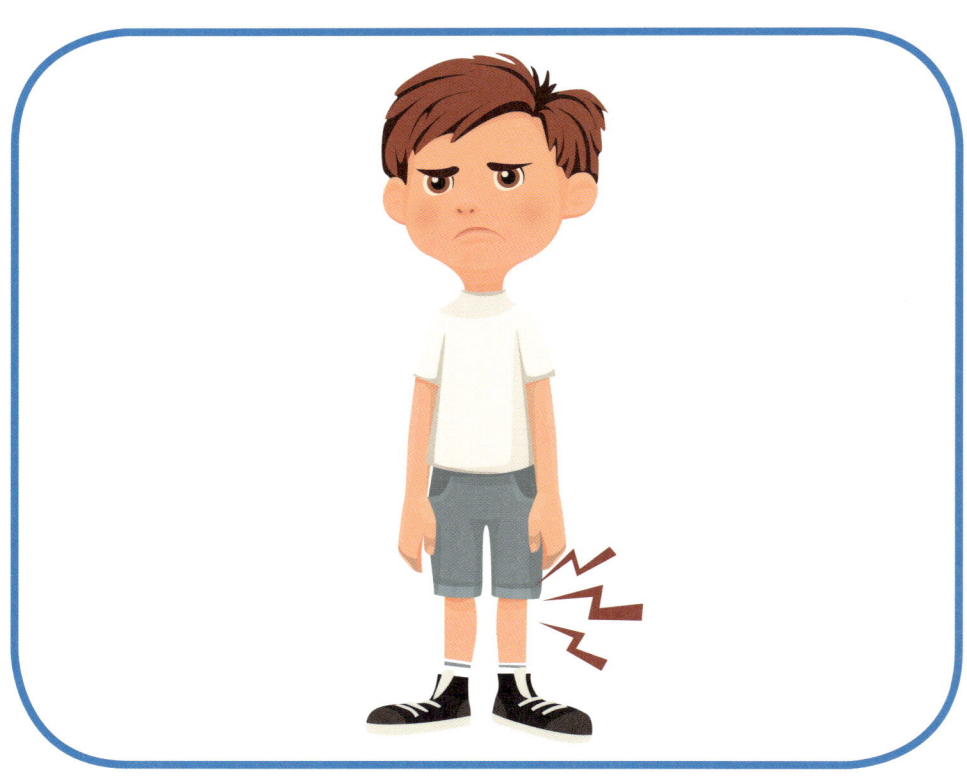

My knee.

My knee hurts.

Where does it hurt?

My finger.

My finger hurts.

Where does it hurt?

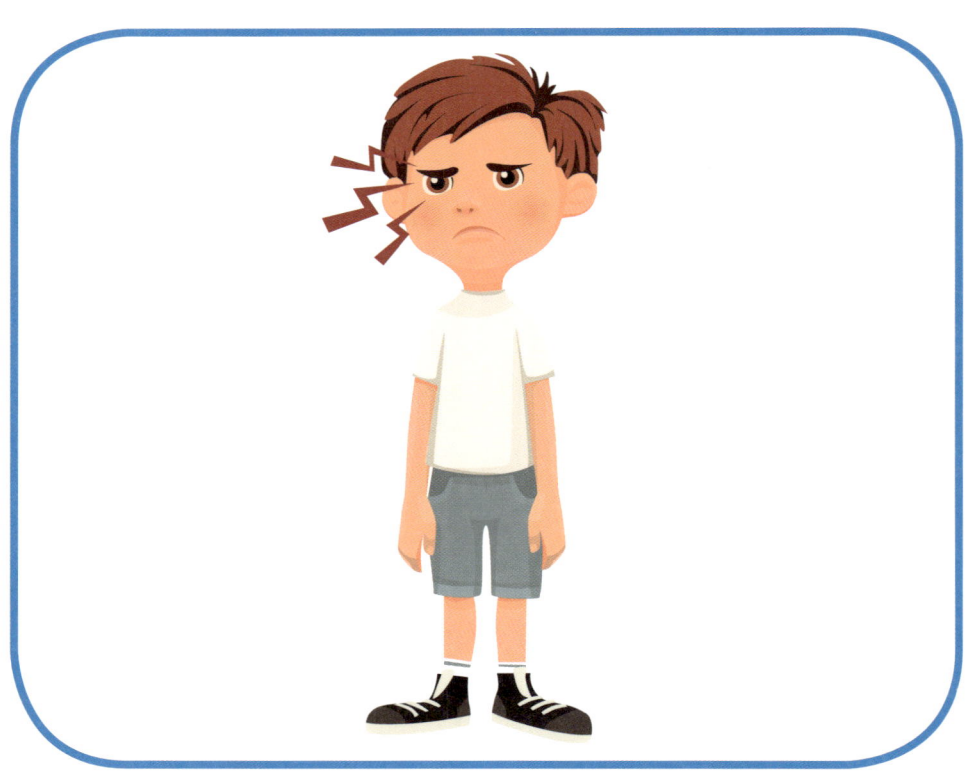

My eye.

My eye hurts.

Where does it hurt?

My ear.

My ear hurts.

Let's learn more about Cinco de Mayo.

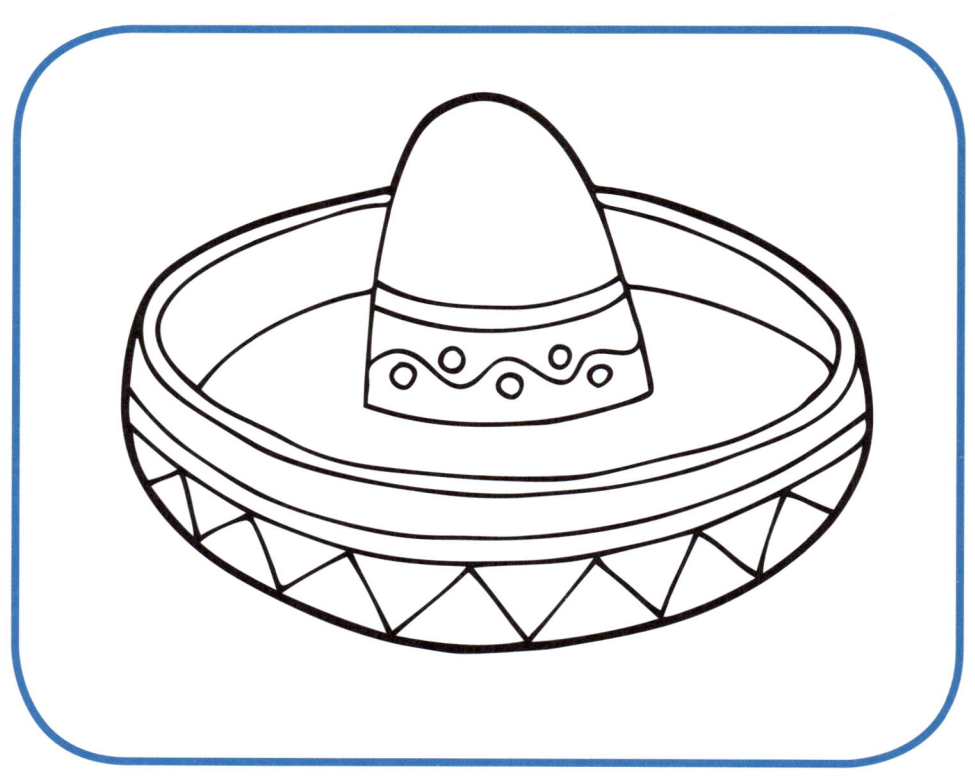

Color the sombrero.